THE NEW BEST OF
NEIL YOUNG
FOR GUITAR

Arranged by Adam Levy

Editor: Colgan Bryan
Book Design: Joseph Klucar
Photography: Roberto Santos

CONTENTS

AFTER THE GOLD RUSH

Words and Music by
NEIL YOUNG

*Piano arr. for fingerstyle gtr.

dreamed I saw the knights in ar - mor com - ing, say - in' some - thing a - bout the queen.
2.3. See additional lyrics

After the Gold Rush - 4 - 1
PG9620

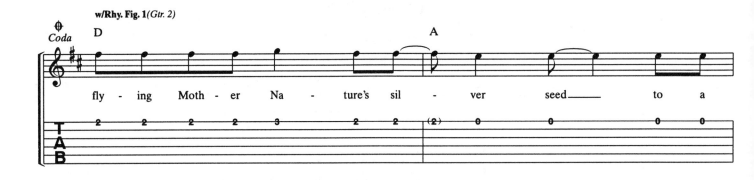

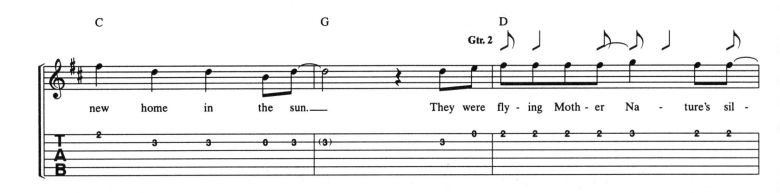

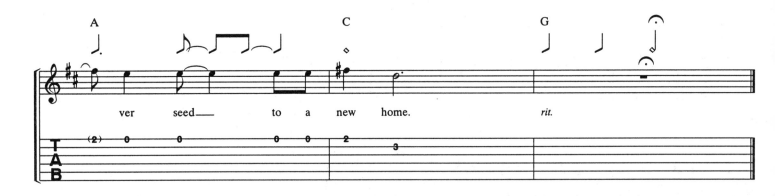

Verse 2:
I was lyin' in a burned out basement
With the full moon in my eyes.
I was hopin' for replacement
When the sun burst through the sky.
There was a band playin' in my head
And I felt like getting high.
I was thinkin' about what a friend had said,
I was hopin' it was a lie.

Verse 3:
Well, I dreamed I saw the silver space ships flyin'
In the yellow haze of the sun,
There were children cryin' and colors flyin'
All around the chosen ones.
All in a dream, all in a dream
The loading had begun.
They were flying Mother Nature's silver seed
To new home in the sun.

ALABAMA

Words and Music by
NEIL YOUNG

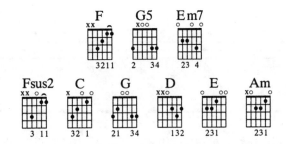

8

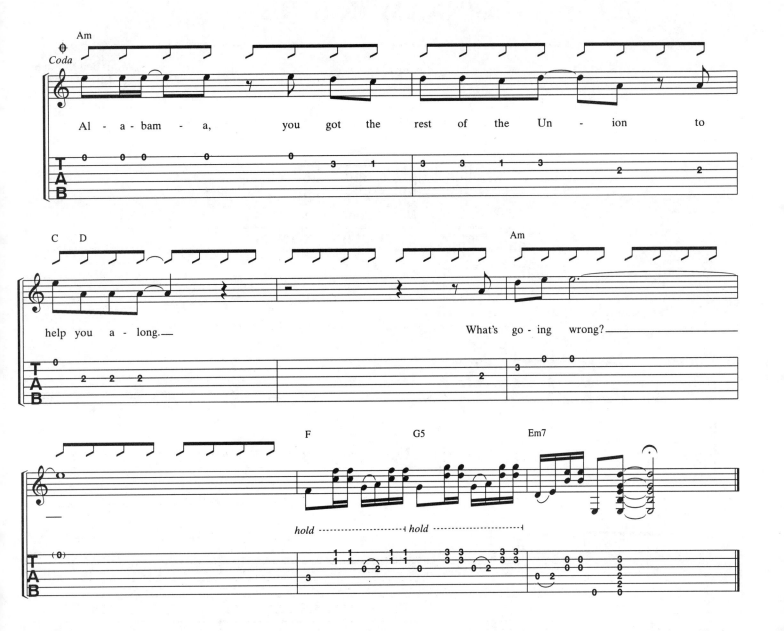

Verse 2:
Oh, Alabama;
Banjos plaing through the broken glass.
Windows down in Alabama.
See the old folks tied up in white ropes;
Hear the banjo; don't it take you down home?
(To Chorus:)

Verse 3:
Oh, Alabama;
Can I see you and shake your hand?
Make friends down in Alabama;
I'm from a new land; I come to you and see all this ruin.
What are you doin'?
Alabama, you got the rest of the Union to help you along.
What's goin' wrong?
(To Chorus:)

CINNAMON GIRL

Words and Music by
NEIL YOUNG

Gtr. 1 tuning:
⑥=D ③=G
⑤=A ②=B
④=D ①=D

Moderate rock ♩ = 104

Cinnamon Girl - 3 - 1
PG9620

FROM HANK TO HENDRIX

Words and Music by
NEIL YOUNG

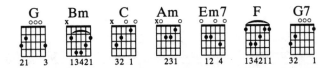

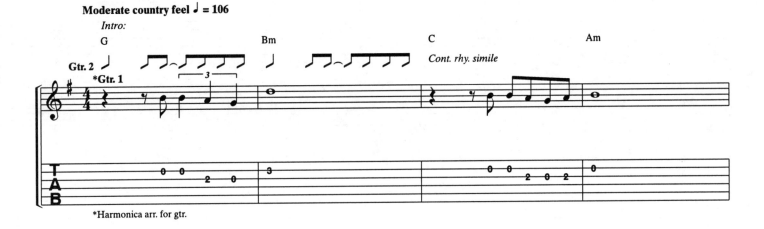

*Harmonica arr. for gtr.

1. From Hank to Hen - drix,— I walked these streets with you.—
2. From Mar-i-lyn to Ma - don-na,— I al - ways loved your smile.—
3. *See additional lyrics*

From Hank To Hendrix - 3 - 1
PG9620

Verse 3:
Sometimes it's distorted, not clear to you.
Sometimes the beauty of love just comes ringin' through.
New glass in the window, new leaf on the tree.
New distance between us, you and me.

HARVEST MOON

Words and Music by
NEIL YOUNG

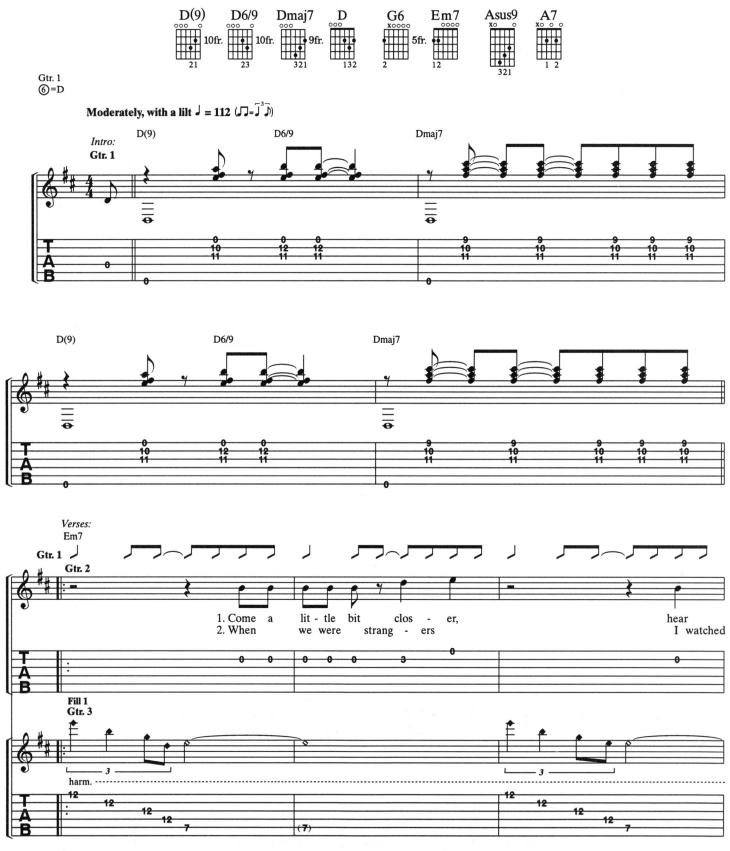

Harvest Moon - 5 - 1
PG9620

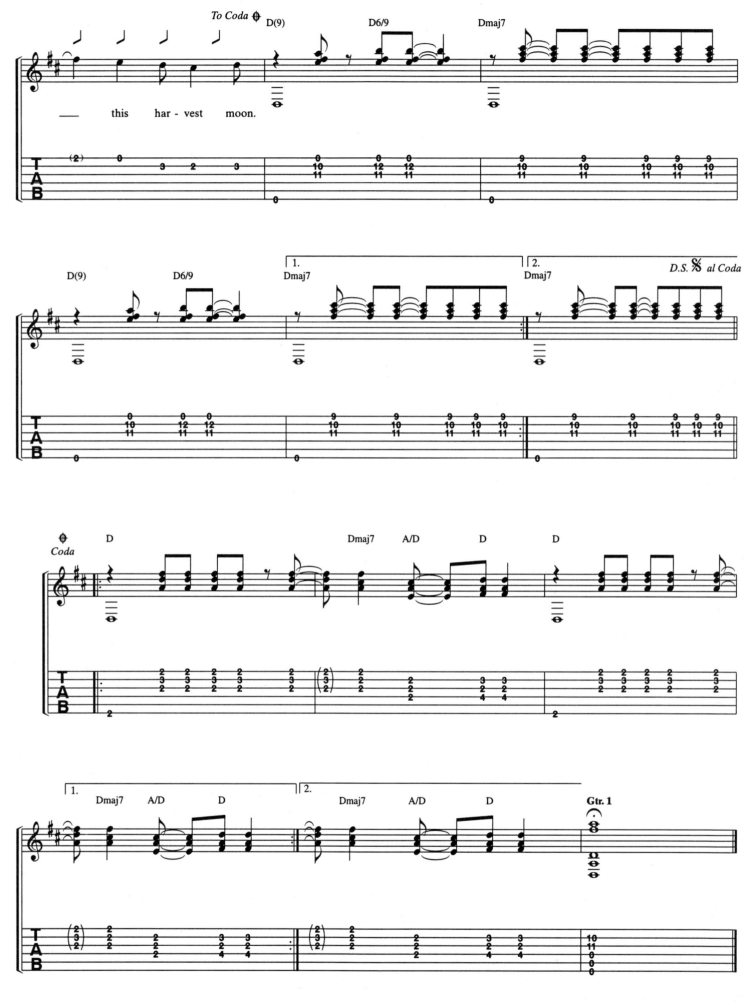

this har-vest moon.

LIKE A HURRICANE

Words and Music by
NEIL YOUNG

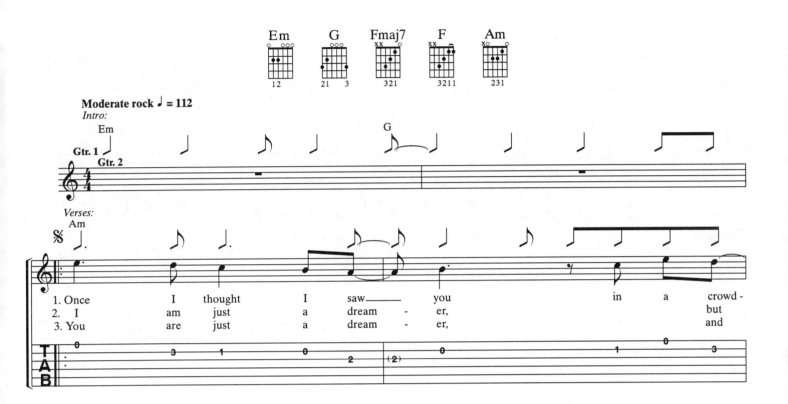

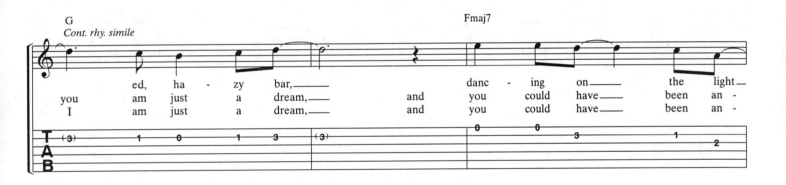

Like a Hurricane - 3 - 1
PG9620

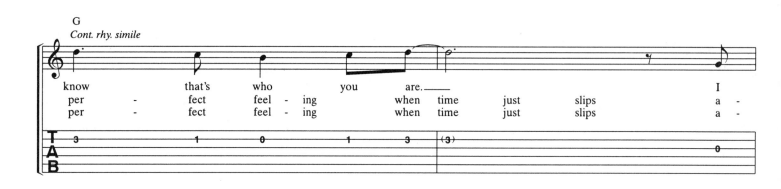

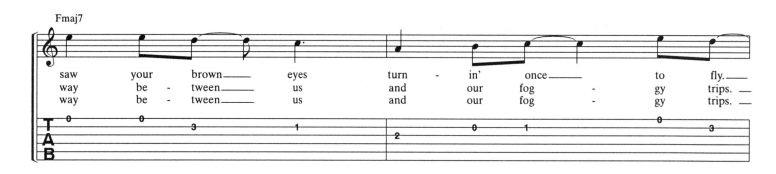

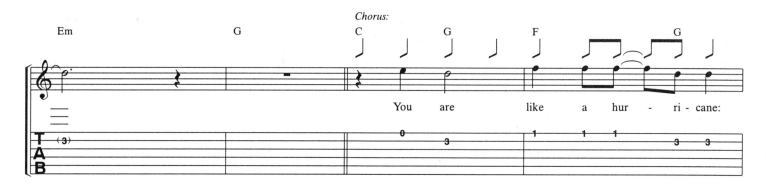

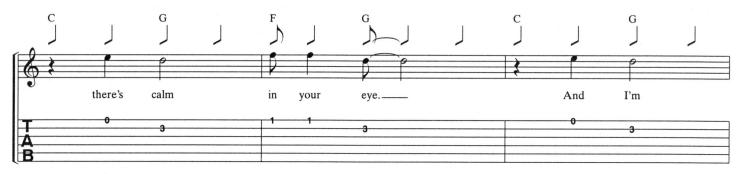

Like a Hurricane - 3 - 3
PG9620

HEART OF GOLD

Words and Music by
NEIL YOUNG

THE NEEDLE AND THE DAMAGE DONE

Words and Music by
NEIL YOUNG

OHIO

OLD MAN

**Words and Music by
NEIL YOUNG**

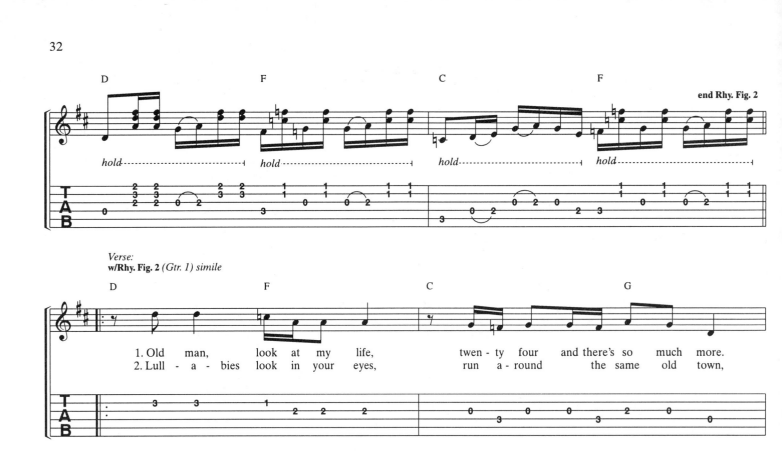

Verse:
w/Rhy. Fig. 2 *(Gtr. 1) simile*

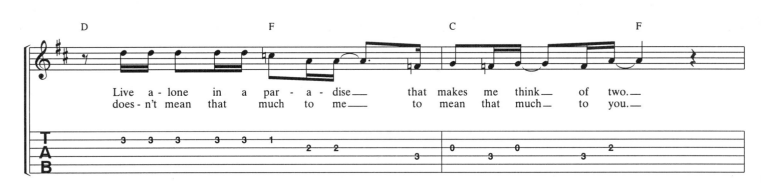

1. Old man, look at my life, twen - ty four and there's so much more.
2. Lull - a - bies look in your eyes, run a - round the same old town,

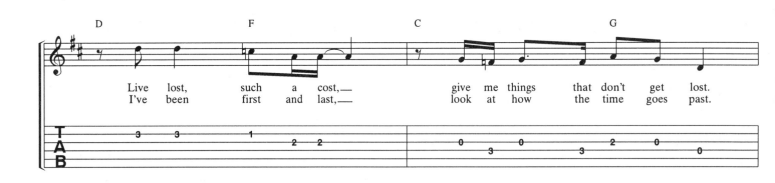

Live a - lone in a par - a - dise___ that makes me think___ of two.___
does - n't mean that much to me___ to mean that much___ to you.___

Live lost, such a cost,___ give me things that don't get lost.
I've been first and last,___ look at how the time goes past.

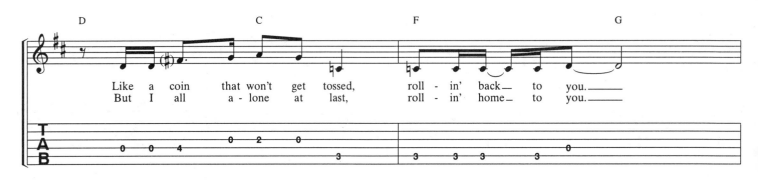

Like a coin that won't get tossed, roll - in' back___ to you.___
But I all a - lone at last, roll - in' home___ to you.___

ONLY LOVE CAN BREAK YOUR HEART

Words and Music by
NEIL YOUNG

Only Love Can Break Your Heart - 2 - 1
PG9620

SOUTHERN MAN

Words and Music by
NEIL YOUNG

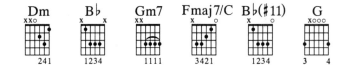

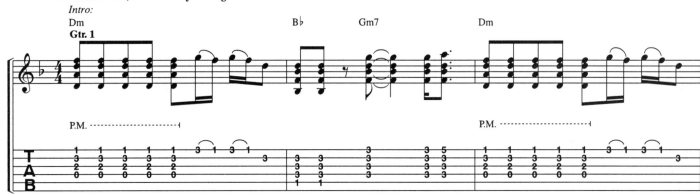

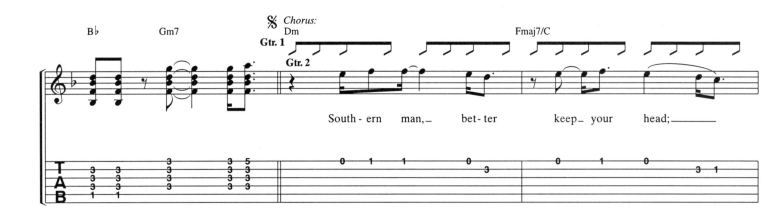

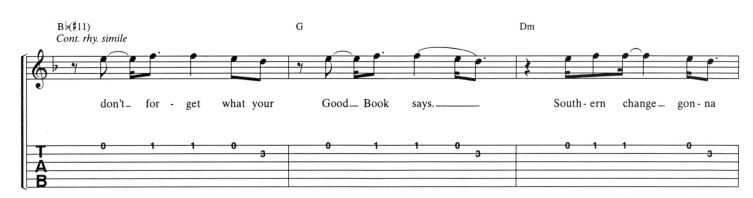

Southern Man - 3 - 1
PG9620

GUITAR TAB GLOSSARY **

TABLATURE EXPLANATION

READING TABLATURE: Tablature illustrates the six strings of the guitar. Notes and chords are indicated by the placement of fret numbers on a given string(s).

String ⑥, 3rd Fret   *String ① 12th Fret*   A "C" Chord   C Chord Arpeggiated
                        String ③ 13th Fret

BENDING NOTES

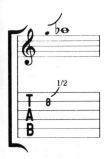

HALF STEP: Play the note and bend string one half step.*

PREBEND AND RELEASE: Bend the string, play it, then release to the original note.

WHOLE STEP: Play the note and bend string one whole step.

RHYTHM SLASHES

STRUM INDICA-TIONS: Strum with indicated rhythm. The chord voicings are found on the first page of the transcription underneath the song title.

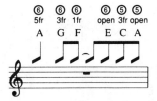

INDICATING SINGLE NOTES USING RHYTHM SLASHES: Very often single notes are incorporated into a rhythm part. The note name is indicated above the rhythm slash with a fret number and a string indication.

*A half step is the smallest interval in Western music; it is equal to one fret. A whole step equals two frets.

**By Kenn Chipkin and Aaron Stang

ARTICULATIONS

HAMMER ON: Play lower note, then "hammer on" to higher note with another finger. Only the first note is attacked.

PULL OFF: Play higher note, then "pull off" to lower note with another finger. Only the first note is attacked.

LEGATO SLIDE: Play note and slide to the following note. (Only first note is attacked).

PALM MUTE: The note or notes are muted by the palm of the pick hand by lightly touching the string(s) near the bridge.

ACCENT: Notes or chords are to be played with added emphasis.

DOWN STROKES AND UPSTROKES: Notes or chords are to be played with either a downstroke (⊓ ·) or upstroke (∨) of the pick.

Most guitarists have — or want to have — one foot in the traditional scene and one foot in the contemporary scene. This method addresses both styles with charismatic flair AND solid pedagogy.

Most teachers want to teach according to the needs of individual students. With all the options in Belwin's 21st Century Guitar Library, teachers have it all!

classical ■ rock ■ pop ■ folk
lead guitar ■ rock rhythm
standard notation and tablature
accompaniments
blues and rock riffs ■ power chords
lead scales
note reading ■ creativity
lesson plans ■ performance tips
fretboard understanding
musicianship

Available from your favorite music dealer:

LEVEL 1
(EL 03842) Guitar Method 1
(EL 03842AT) Guitar Method 1 w/Cassette
(EL 03842CD) Guitar Method 1 w/CD
(EL 03851AT) Guitar Rock Shop 1 w/Cassette
(EL 03851CD) Guitar Rock Shop 1 w/CD
(EL 03845) Guitar Theory 1
(EL 03848AT) Guitar Song Trax 1 w/Cassette
(EL 03848CD) Guitar Song Trax 1 w/CD
(EL 03955S) Guitar Ensemble Student Book 1
(EL 03955AT) Guitar Ensemble Score Book 1
  w/Cassette
(EL 03955CD) Guitar Ensemble Score Book 1
  w/CD
(EL 03960) Guitar Teacher Edition 1

LEVEL 2
(EL 03843) Guitar Method 2
(EL 03843AT) Guitar Method 2 w/Cassette
(EL 03843CD) Guitar Method 2 w/CD
(EL 03852AT) Guitar Rock Shop 2 w/Cassette
(EL 03852CD) Guitar Rock Shop 2 w/CD
(EL 03846) Guitar Theory 2
(EL 03849AT) Guitar Song Trax 2 w/Cassette
(EL 03849CD) Guitar Song Trax 2 w/CD
(EL 03957S) Guitar Ensemble Student Book 2
(EL 03957AT) Guitar Ensemble Score Book 2
  w/Cassette
(EL 03957CD) Guitar Ensemble Score Book 2
  w/CD
(EL 03961) Guitar Teacher Edition 2

Level 3 coming soon